Bible Stories for....

Early Readers

Level 2
Book 4

7 Dips
Naaman Finds a Cure
2 Kings 5:1-16

By Lavaun Linde
Mary Quishenberry
Illustrated by
Joe Maniscalco

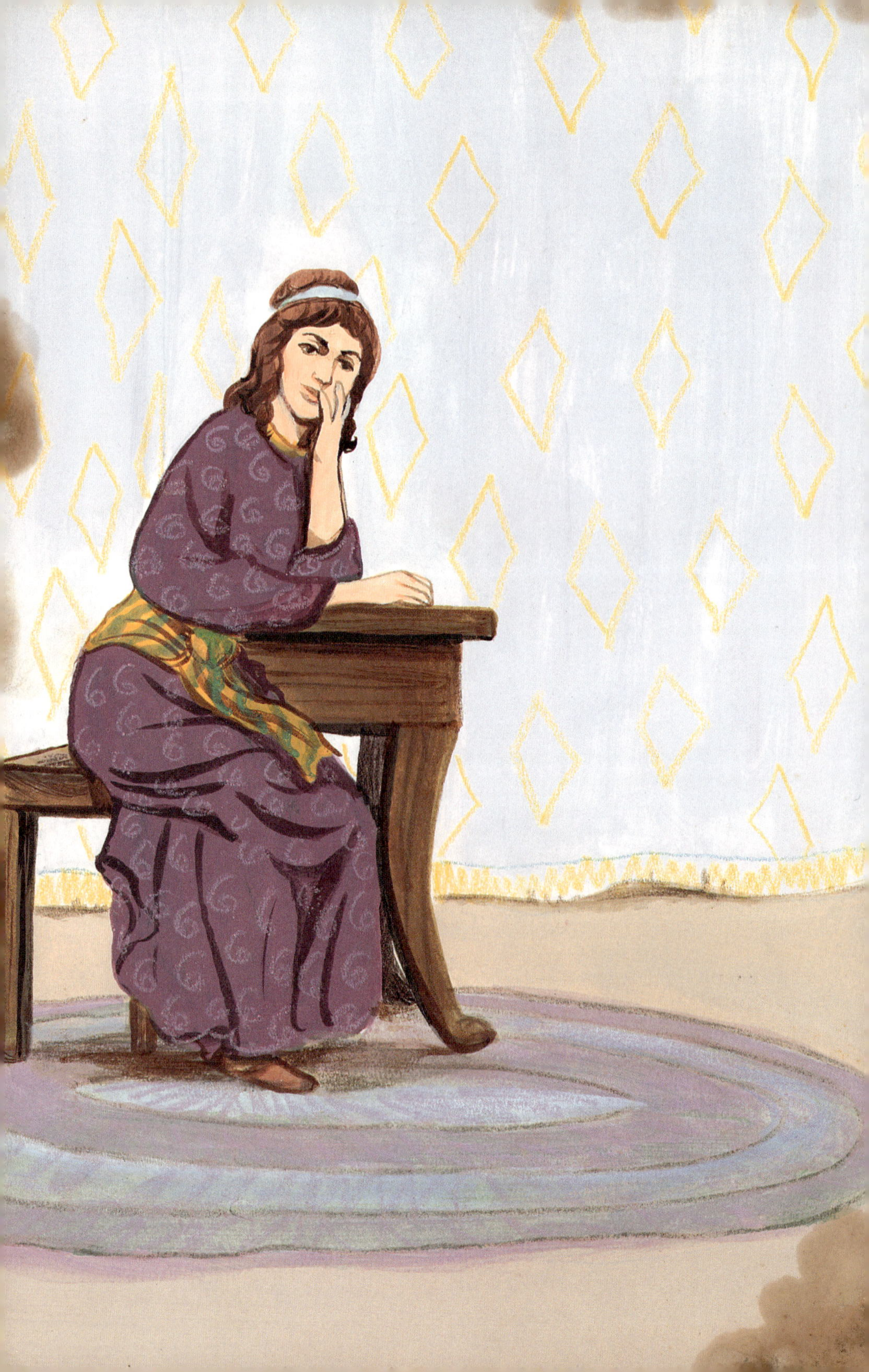

"I am a slave
in a land miles and miles
from Mom and Dad.
I can not go home,
but God will take care of me."

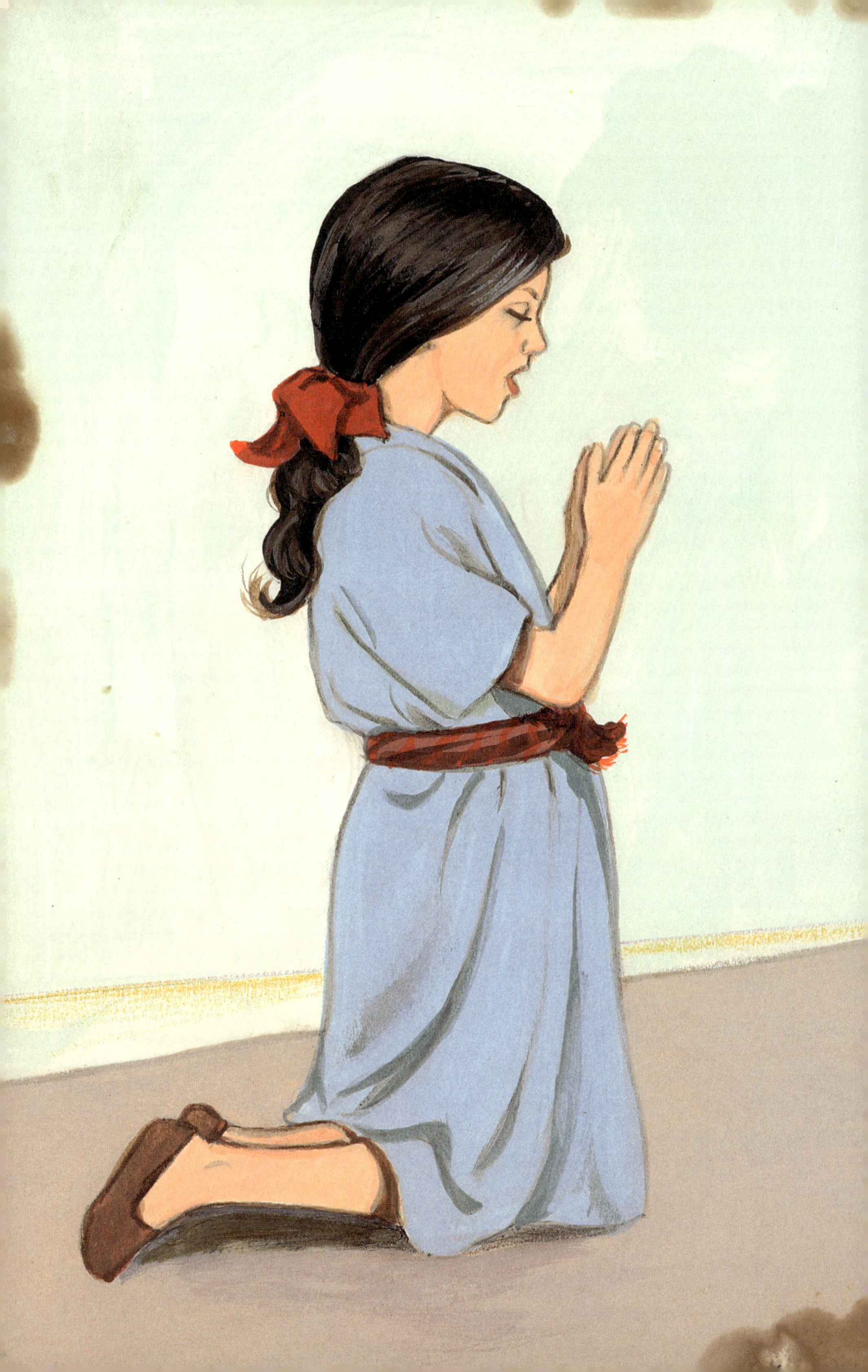

"It is a big job
to take care
of Naaman
and his wife's home,"
the girl prays to God.
"Help me
with this job.
And help Naaman
and his wife
to love You."

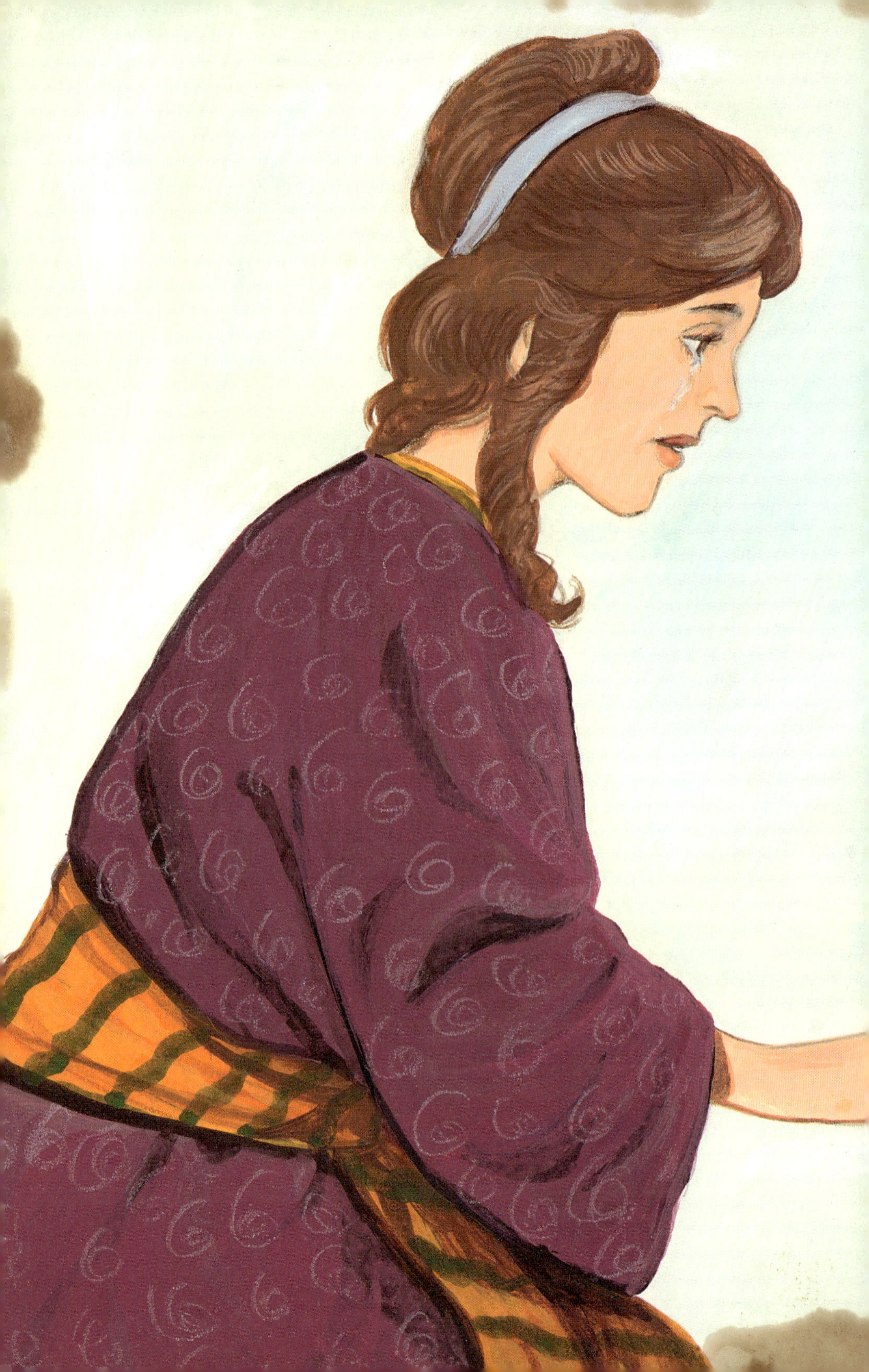

Naaman's wife tells the girl,
"Naaman has white spots
on him.
He is sick. I am sad."

"The man of God
can make
Naaman well,"
the girl tells
Naaman's wife.

Naaman and his men go
to see the man of God.
Naaman tells himself,
"The man of God will see me
and make me well."

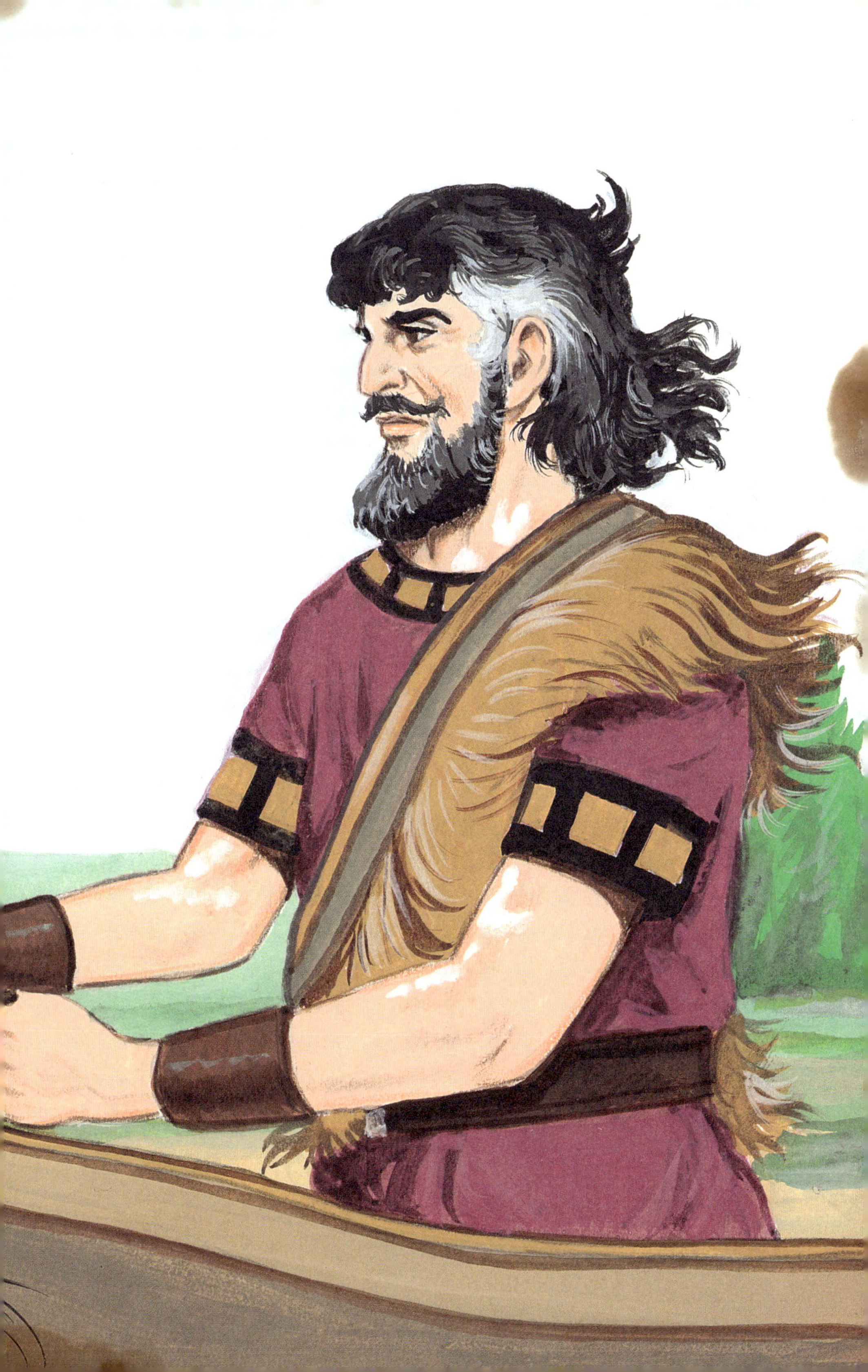

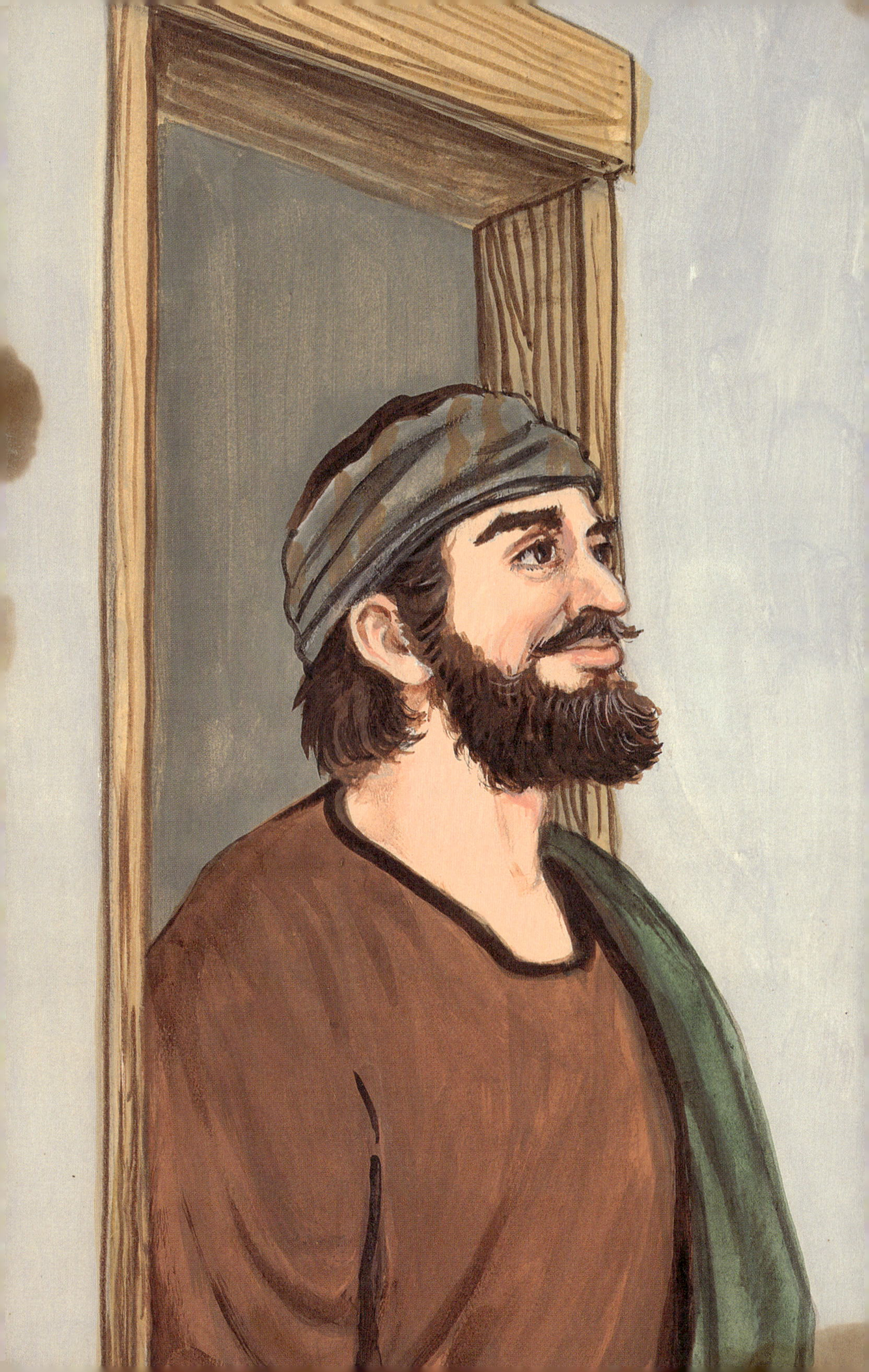

But the man of God sends his helper to see Naaman. The helper tells Naaman, "Go to the river. Dip in it 7 times, and God will make you well."

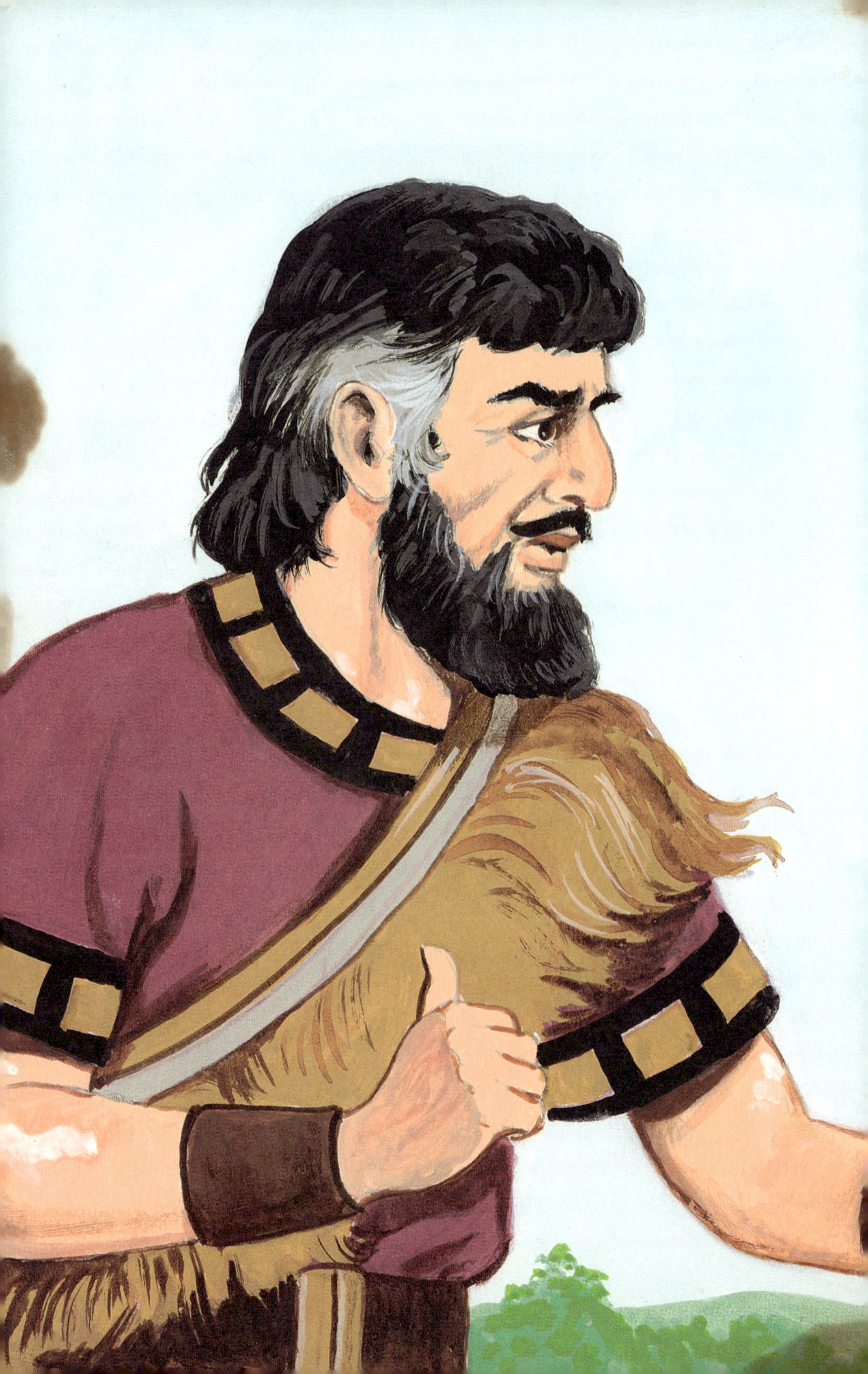

"What! The man of God
will not take the time
to see me and make me well!"
Naaman tells his men.
"And what is more,
I am to go
and dip
in that river.
I will not
go!"

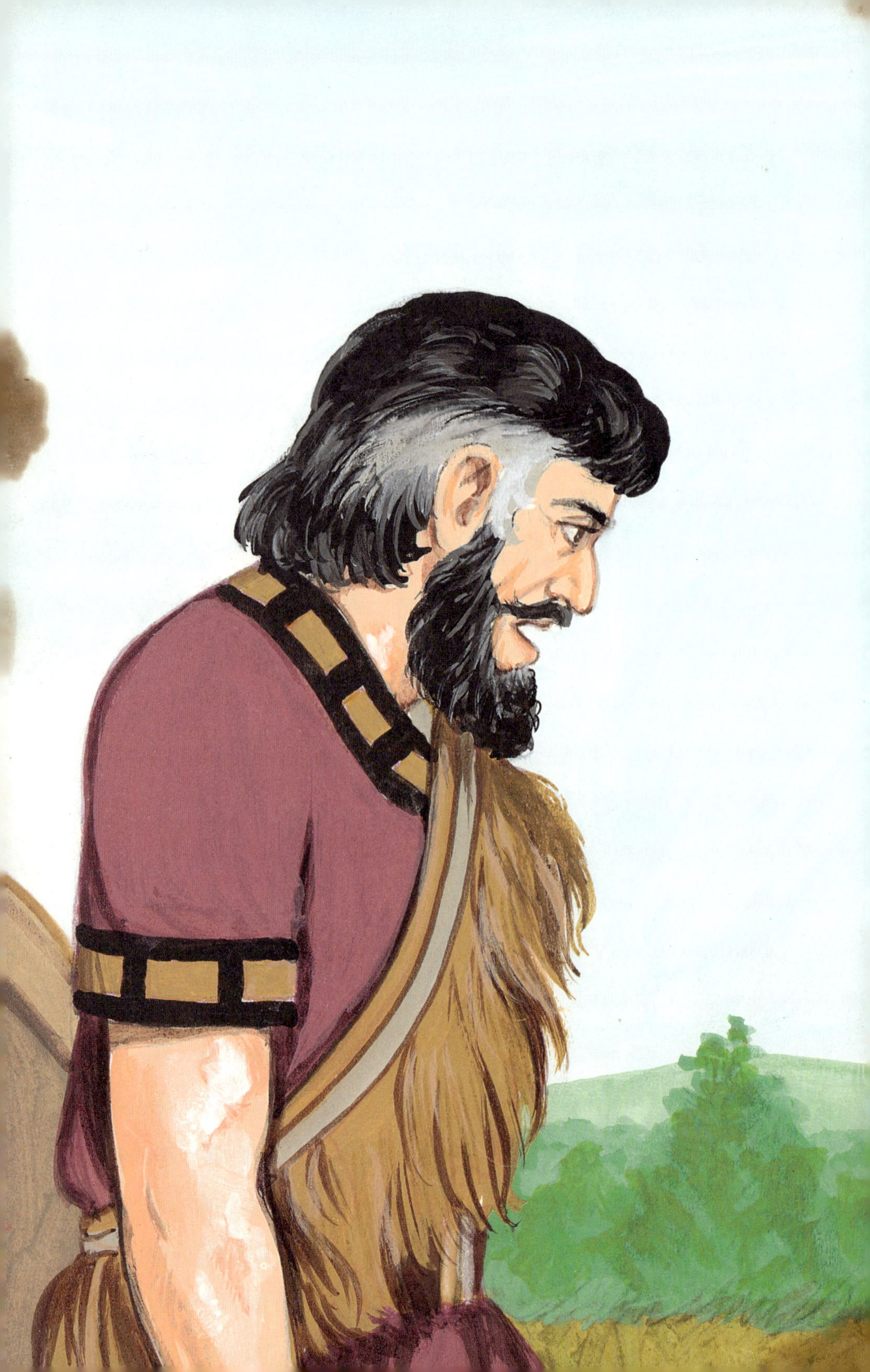

"Let us go to the river."

"No! It has mud.
It is not fit for a dip."

"Come on
so you
can get well!"

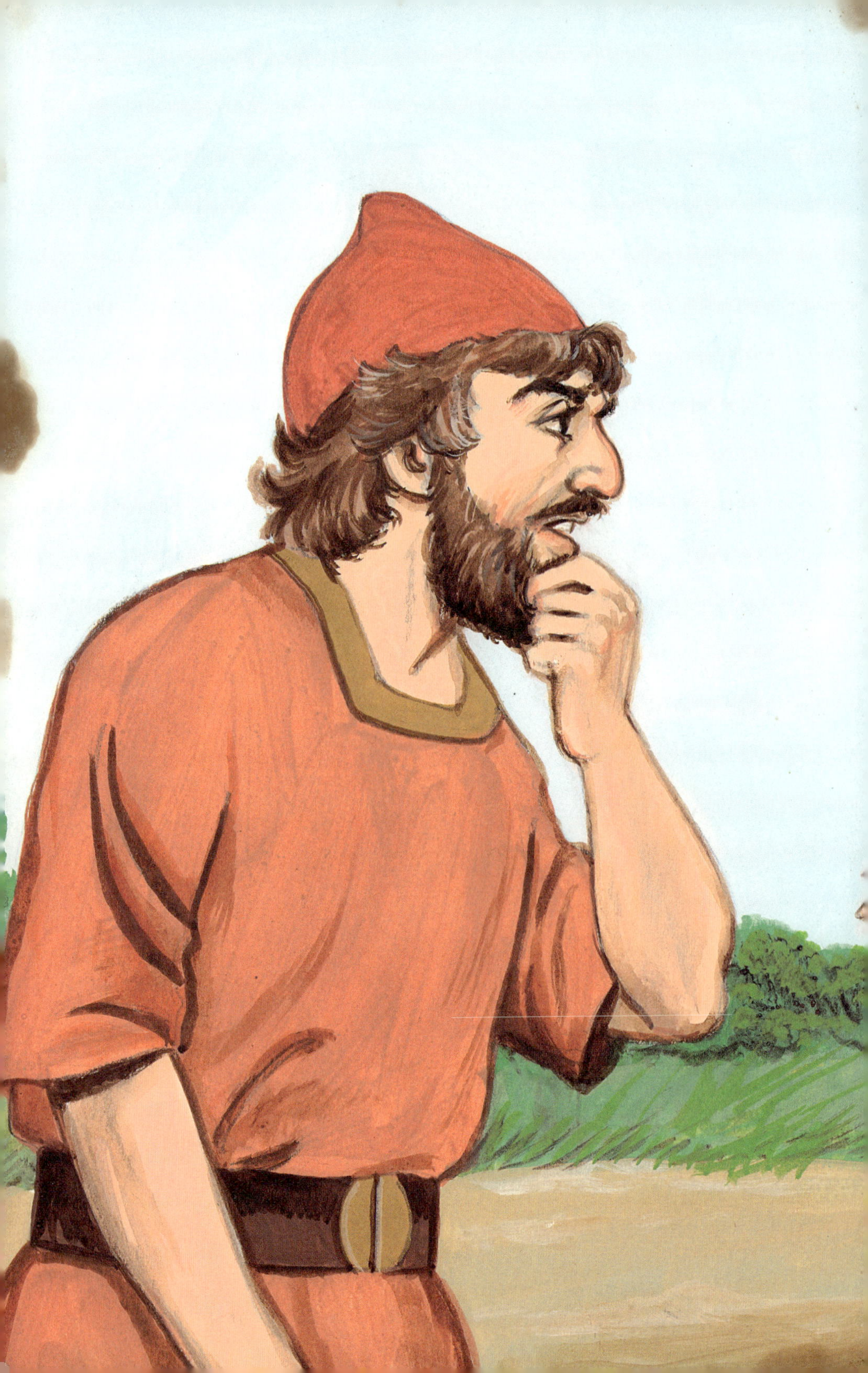

At last Naaman tells his men, "I—will—go."

Naaman dips in the river 1 time.
He has spots.

2 times.
He has spots.
Naaman dips
3, 4, 5, 6 times
and he
still has the spots.

"Just one more dip in the river!"
Naaman makes his last dip.
"I am well! I am well!"
Naaman yells.

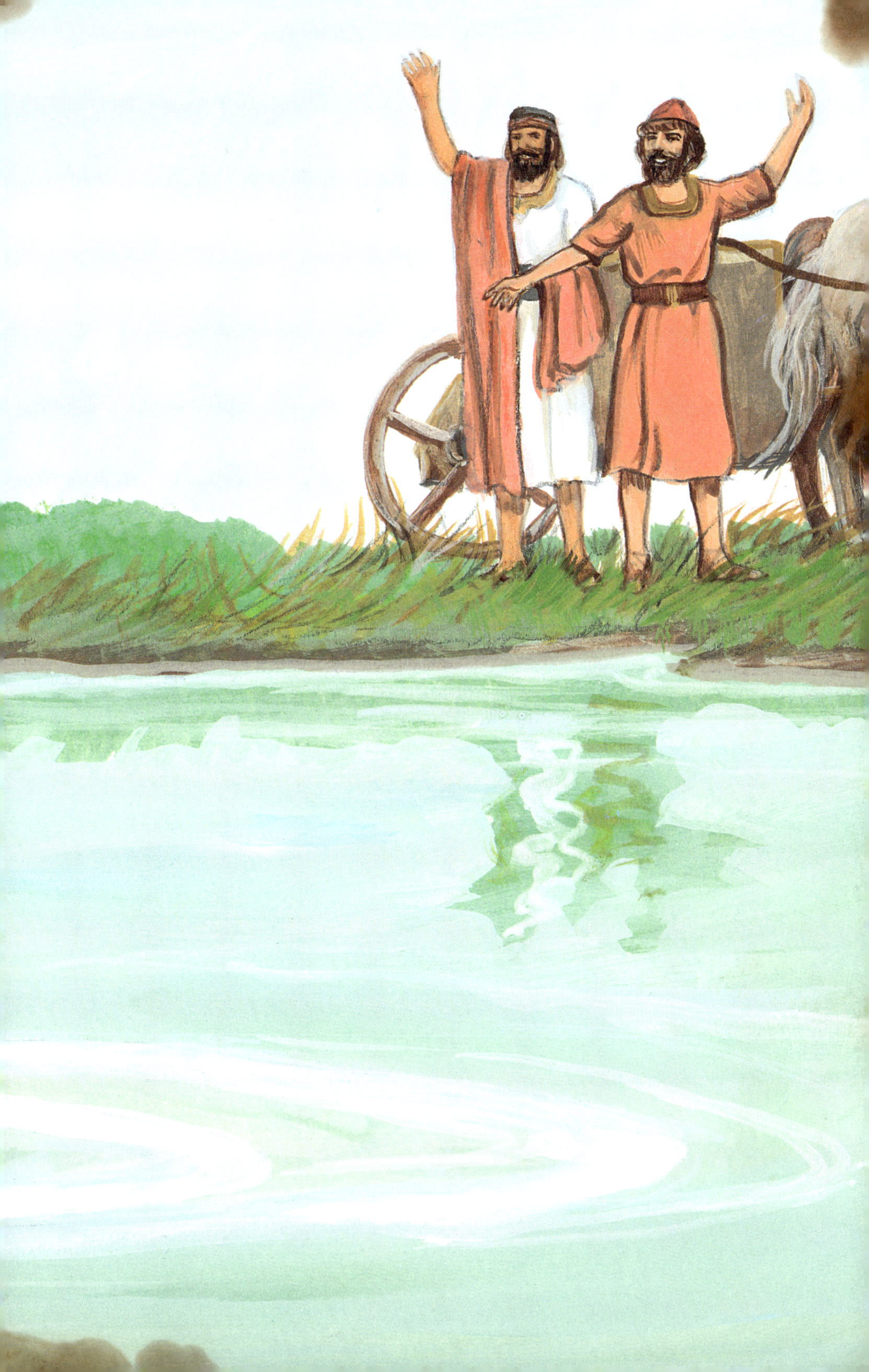

Naaman rides back to see the man of God. "Thank you! Thank you!" Naaman tells him.

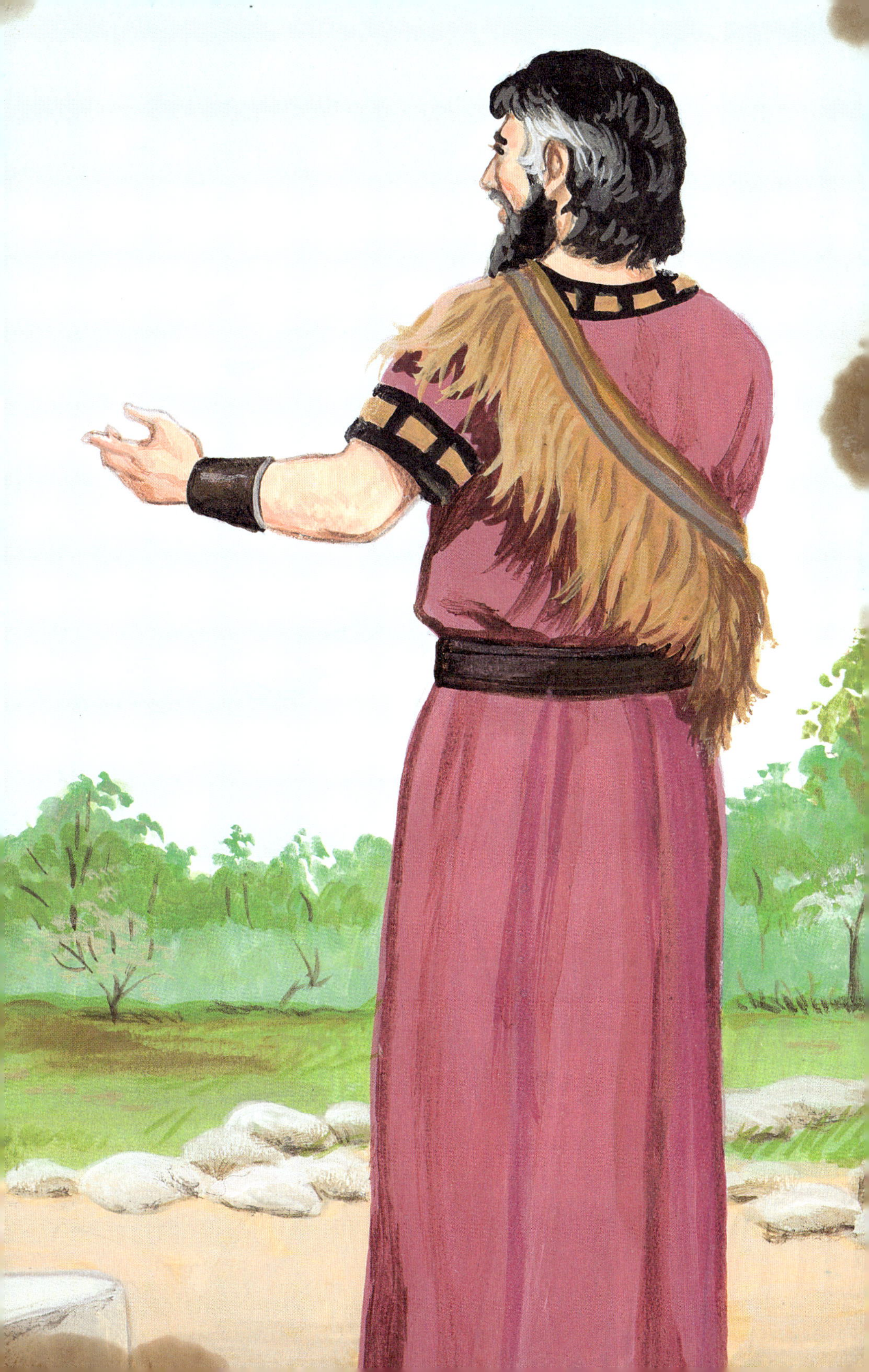

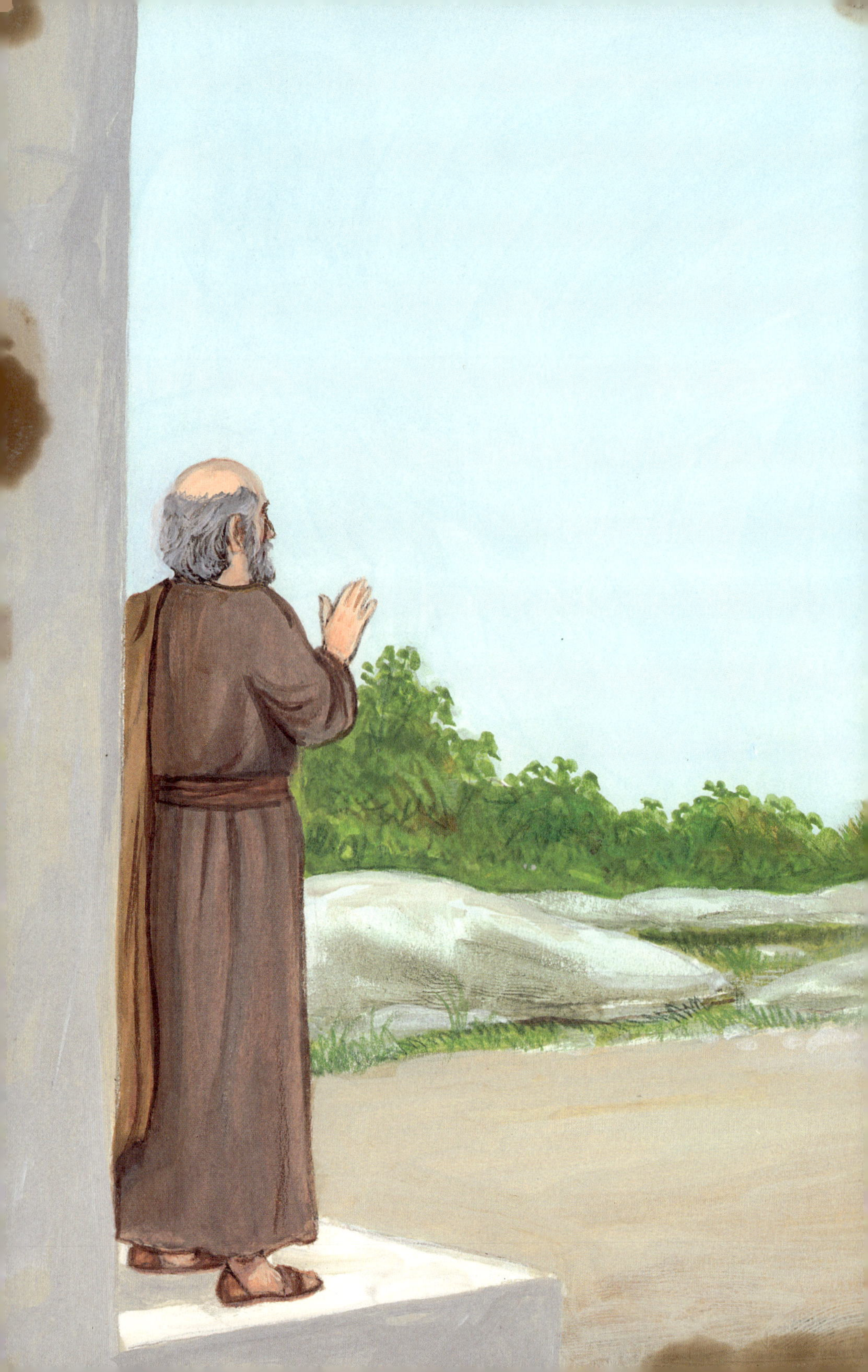

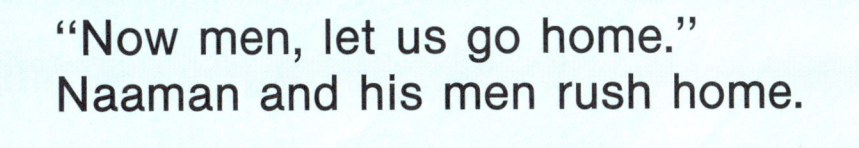

"Now men, let us go home."
Naaman and his men rush home.

"I am well!"
Naaman yells
to his wife and the girl.

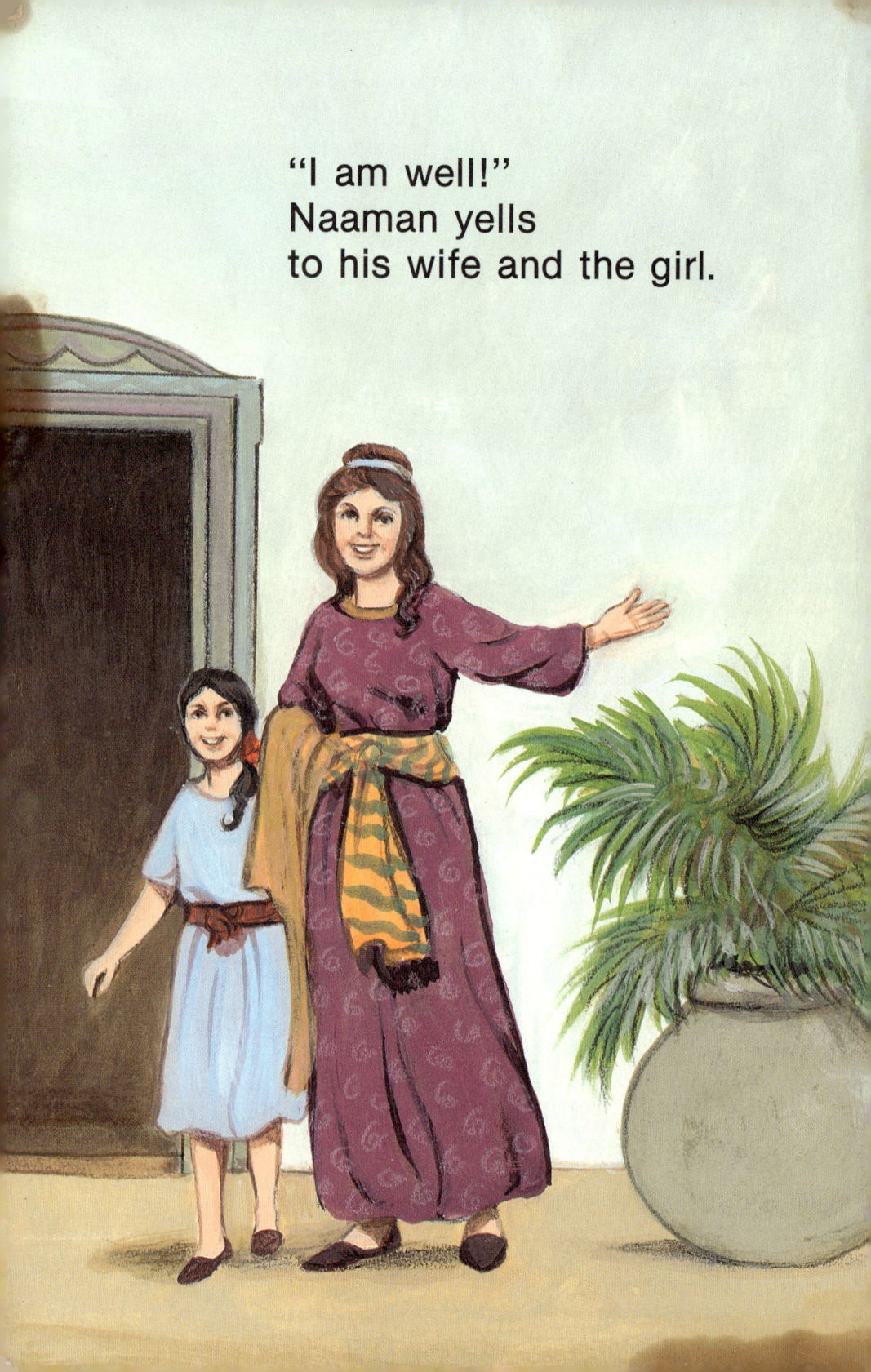

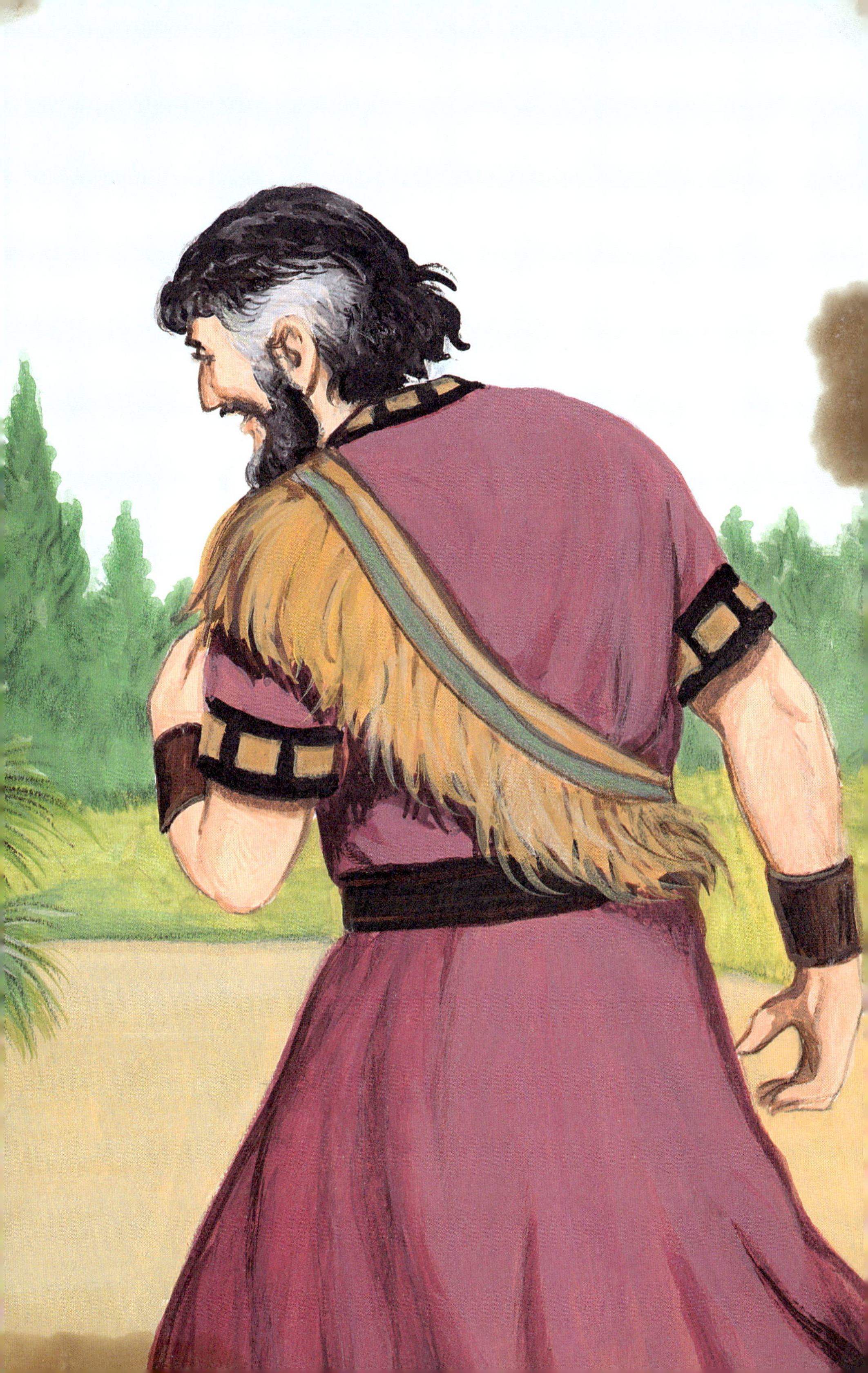

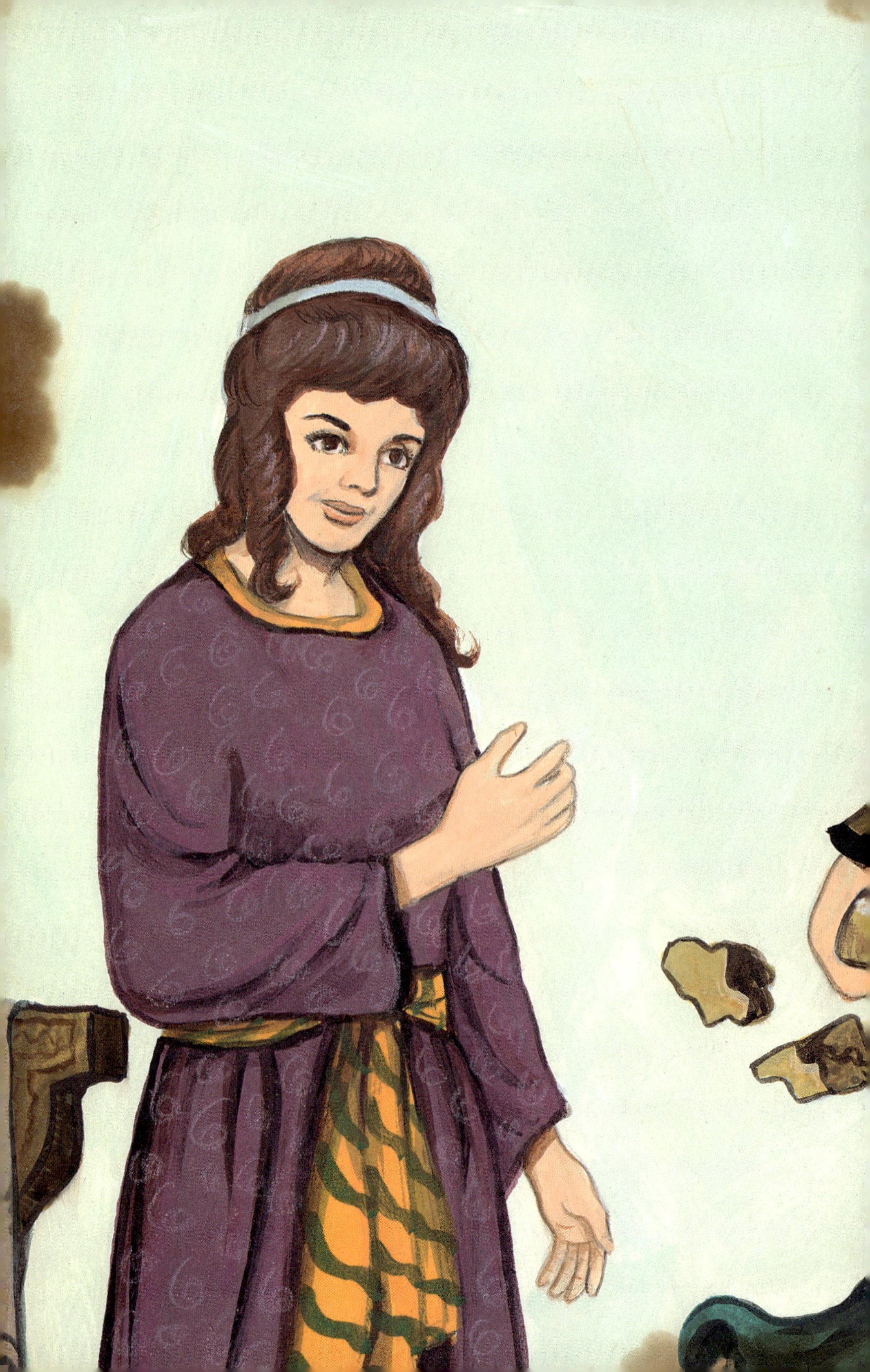

"The girl's God made me well!" Naaman tells his wife. Naaman and his wife are so glad! "No more fake gods for us!"

The girl prays to God,
"I love You
and I am glad
that You made Naaman well.
I am so glad
Naaman and his wife
love You now!
Thank You, God."

God has a promise
for me in James 5:15.

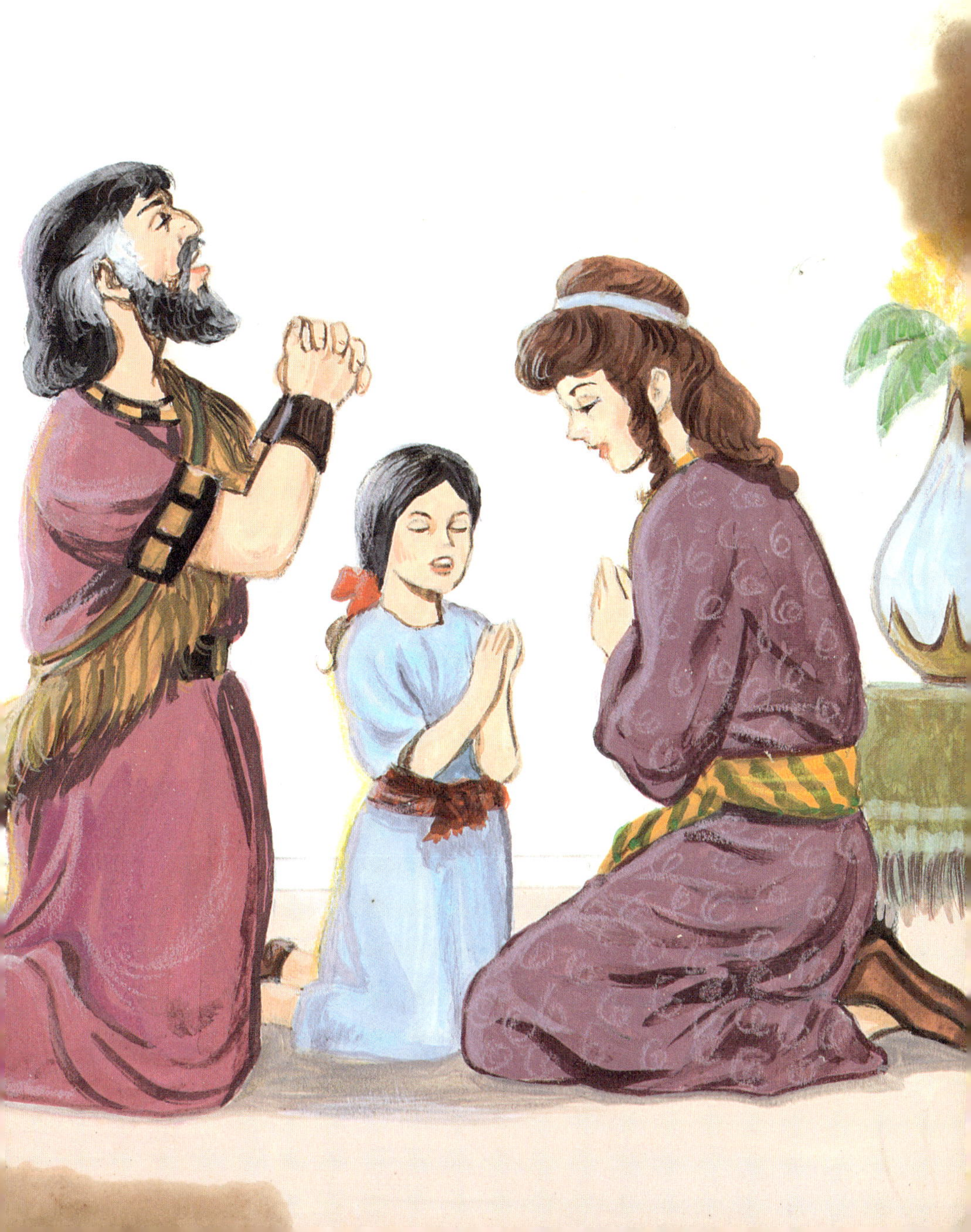

Something to Think About

1. The slave girl had to work day after day. Who did she ask to help her?

2. How did Naaman and his wife feel about having a slave girl that loved the true God?

3. What can I do to be a missionary like the slave girl?